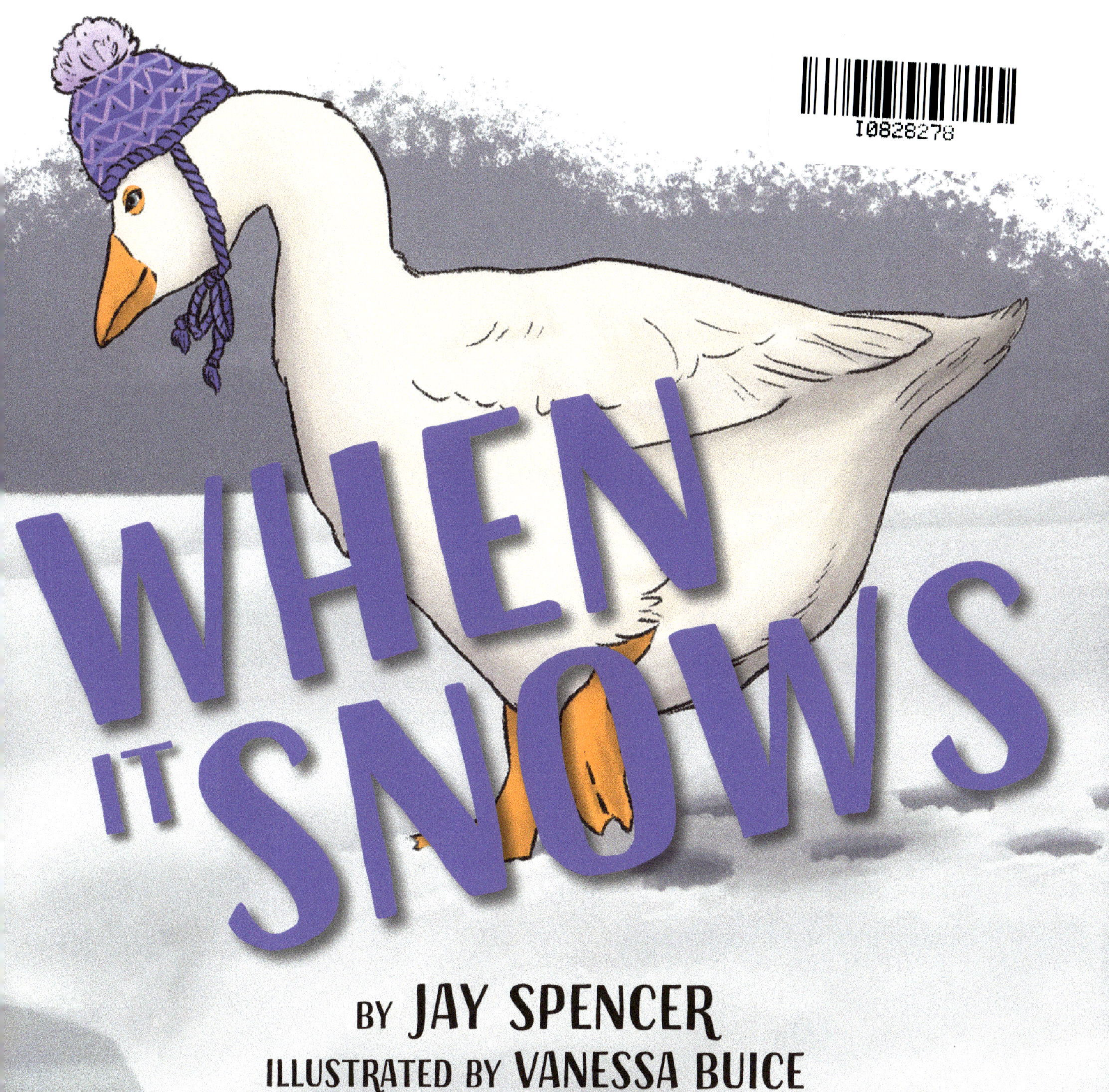
When It Snows
By Jay Spencer
Illustrated by Vanessa Buice
I0828278

Editor: Amy Ashby

ISBN: 978-1-7358600-2-2 (hard cover)
ISBN: 978-1-7358600-3-9 (soft cover)

Published by Warren Publishing
Charlotte, NC
www.warrenpublishing.net
Printed in the United States

*Dedicated to my wife and family
for their love and support.*

WHEN IT SNOWS...

Does a snowshoe hare get under a blanket to cuddle?

Carrying it around would be so much trouble.

NOOO...

Her short, brown hair becomes dense, thick, and white.

When it snows, she'll be warm, hidden, and out of sight.

WHEN IT SNOWS...

Does a goose put a toboggan
over his tiny, little brain?

Keeping it tied would
be such a strain.

NOOO...

He flies down south under
the light of the moon.

With the wind behind him,
he will be there soon.

WHEN IT SNOWS...

Does a moose remove his
antlers to shelter his back?

He would need some help,
but nobody's got time for that!

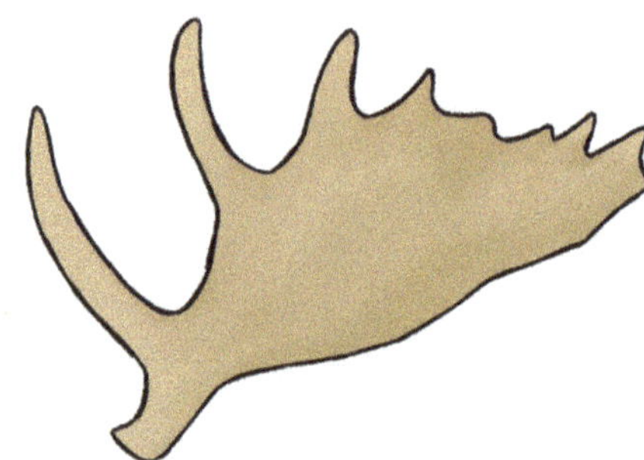

NOOO...

He eats lots of food
all summer long.

So when the weather turns bad,
he will be healthy and strong.

WHEN IT SNOWS...

Does a bear turn on a
heater inside of his den?

If the other animals found out,
they would all want in!

NOOO...

He hibernates under a log
until it warms up in spring.

He doesn't wake up till
the birds begin to sing.

WHEN IT SNOWS...

Does a badger build a fire
to avoid being cold?

Surely the match would
be hard to hold.

NOOO...

He digs a small hole and
burrows in the ground.

Now he and his family
can be safe and sound.

When it's freezing cold
and snow is coming down,

all God's creatures
are safe and sound.

ABOUT THE ILLUSTRATOR

Vanessa Buice attends Rhode Island School of Design. When she's not busy doing school work, she enjoys drawing, reading, being with friends, and snuggling with her pets.

www.ingramcontent.com/pod-product-compliance
Lightning Source LLC
LaVergne TN
LVHW060628110826
845147LV00015B/966

* 9 7 8 1 7 3 5 8 6 0 0 3 9 *